The Gift of Wonder

Story by **Lisa Bear Goldman**

Illustrations by **Patrice Schooley**

YAFOOR YAFOOR YAFOOR YAFOOR YAFOOR YAFOOR

Buddy heard his mother bray loudly as he chased his friend Diego around the corral. The morning air was cool and Buddy, the little donkey, and Diego, the young mule, ran hard as they played their game of tag. "Yafoor," she called again. Buddy skidded to a stop.

She only called him by his birth name if he was in trouble or she had something very serious to tell him. Little Buddy trotted toward her. Was he in trouble? Had he done something to dishonor her, or his herd, without knowing? He stood nervously by her side and looked up at her. His mother stood proudly and her eyes shone brightly.

"My son," she said, "Raven has chosen you to be in this year's Animal Messenger Parade." Buddy heard her words but could not believe it.

Every year Raven picked some of the animals to be in the parade, and then one was chosen to be a messenger to the humans or "two-leggeds." The animals had an important message for the two-leggeds and it was a great honor to be chosen. Buddy remembered hearing that the message to be delivered had to do with the animals' survival.

Slowly his mother's words started to sink in.
Buddy shook his head to clear his thoughts. Being in
the Animal Messenger Parade didn't mean he would
be chosen to be a messenger, but it was still an honor.
"We must go and get you ready," Buddy's mother said.

Buddy had never been so clean. He even had a flower
tucked behind his ear.

Buddy walked next to his mother. He was so excited he kicked the air, wishing he could run. As they joined the gathering of the animals in the meadow, Buddy's mother told him the story of how he got his birth name. "There is a tale from a far away land of a donkey who could talk to the two-leggeds," she said as she smiled at him. "His name was Yafoor."

Buddy gazed in amazement. He had never seen so many animals in one place. With surprise, he noticed they were all very well behaved.

The fox was not chasing the rabbit, who was sitting quietly at his feet.

The frog sat calmly next to the dragonfly.

Watching the animals gather below
Raven cawed loudly,

"Start the parade Start the parade!"

Buddy got in line with
the other animals and they
began to circle. Buddy thought of
the stories he had heard about
Raven as he walked.

She brought the sun to all the creatures, she was a trickster and she was oh so wise. She must be very wise because only Raven could pick an animal messenger, Buddy thought.

Buddy walked carefully as his mother had told him to do. He held his ears as high as he could and he smiled from the inside out. Buddy told himself not to get his hopes up. There were so many beautiful and wondrous animals in the parade.

Bobcat was strong and majestic.

Deer was graceful and elegant.

Fox was so very smart and cunning.

Buddy caught sight of a hummingbird. Sunlight shone
on the little bird and Buddy thought he saw the
twinkle of the stars and the shining
sun in its sparkling feathers.

He was just a young and funny-looking donkey.
He glanced down at his own dull coat. What chance
did he have of being chosen?

Buddy knew once the messenger was chosen, that animal would meet a two-legged and try to communicate the animals' message. Buddy was getting tired of walking.

The parade was taking *forever!*

Then he felt Raven's eyes on him. He took a deep breath and pushed his ears toward the sky.

Raven stretched her wings and took flight.

He heard the swish of her feathers
as she landed on his back.

He had been chosen!

Buddy could not believe it. The other animals stepped
back and admired him. Buddy had never felt so proud.

Raven led him down a trail away from the other animals.

As they walked she told him what it meant to be a messenger. He was supposed to communicate in some way how precious animals are.

The more she told him, the more questions Buddy had.

How would he know what to do with his two-legged?

How would he pass on the animals' message?

Would he be understood?

Raven told him to look into the eyes of his two-legged and open his heart.

Could it really be that easy?

Suddenly, Raven told him to stop. Buddy looked around, but he did not see a two-legged. Then off in a field he saw a girl. She was throwing something and a dog was chasing it. "There is your two-legged," Raven said as she flew into a tree.

Buddy walked slowly toward the girl. She did not notice him. She was busy playing. He waited and then he waited some more.

How could he be a messenger if she didn't look at him?

Buddy got closer and she still didn't look at him. He had to get her attention.

After thinking about it,

Buddy let out a loud bray.

Both the girl and the dog stopped their play and looked at him in surprise.

Then she burst out laughing. He had her attention all right. She walked over to him and touched his head.

Remembering Raven's words Buddy opened his eyes wide and gazed into her eyes. He took a breath and opened his heart. He felt a warm and tingly feeling growing inside him.

Grinning at the donkey's silly-sounding bray, she spoke, "You are the funniest looking animal ever. Your head, your ears and even your belly are too big for your body." Everything about him made her laugh.

When she finally quit laughing, something drew her to him. As she looked into his large, warm eyes, she felt something very strange happen.

The girl thought she heard her name called and a peaceful feeling came over her. Was this silly donkey smiling at her?

Stroking his cheek, she saw every detail of his face magnified. She saw the colors of his fur. She noticed the straight fringe of his eyelashes and the long curly hair on his forehead. The skin around his mouth was so soft and beautiful it almost made her cry. She watched his nose as he breathed. This little donkey was a miracle.

Time seemed to stand still and her heart filled with the beauty and wonder of this creature. She did not know how long she stood there. When the girl finally lowered her hand from the donkey's head, she knew she was changed.

This animal had given her a precious message and gift. Looking around, everything looked brand new and wondrous. As the girl turned to walk away, she called her dog and smiled at him. He wagged his tail and smiled back at her.

Walking home she wished she could thank this little donkey. She looked over her shoulder and tried to tell him with her eyes. She thought she heard her name called again and this time she was sure he was smiling at her.

Buddy watched the girl walk away.

His heart was so full it felt ready to burst. He heard
Raven call and felt her land on his back.
No words were needed.

He was certain his two-legged would treasure and look
after animals throughout her life.

Buddy smiled from the inside out and even though
Raven was on his back, he gave a joyful kick in the air.

The End

Lisa Bear Goldman is a published children's book author and counselor. She spent her early years in Albuquerque, and Santa Fe, New Mexico, and then attended the University of Arizona in Tucson, Arizona, where she completed her Master's Degree in Rehabilitation Counseling. She currently works as a counselor in New Mexico. In addition to her love of writing, she works as an artist's representative for her father, Herb Goldman, an accomplished sculptor. Lisa is on the Board of Directors of Art Has Heart, JB & Amado Pena's Foundation providing educational scholarships for young people. Lisa's work as a counselor inspired her to write The Gift of Wonder. Her donkey Burrito, aka, Buddy lives with her happily in the mountains of Placitas, New Mexico.

Patrice Schooley received a Fine Arts Degree from the University of New Mexico and began doing juried shows with her watercolors, acrylics and pencil art. Eventually, she found her true passion in painting animals and children and has done commissioned work throughout the United States. Patrice believes in the importance of art for children and has taught many classes both in local schools and in private lessons. She also devotes much of her time to animal rescue work and always donates a portion of her sales to various animal charities. Patrice believes that all animals have many wonderful and magical things to teach humans if we take the time to listen. She would like to thank Burrito for being her model and muse for the illustrations in this book.

A special thanks to *Dana Caruso* for all her help in the design and layout of The Gift of Wonder.

Burrito, aka Buddy, is thrilled with his second book. He hopes this story will inspire children and adults to find the magic and wonder in all creatures great and small.

Library of Congress Control Number: 2014911186

ISBN 978-0-9832074-1-2

www.ingramcontent.com/pod-product-compliance
Lightning Source LLC
LaVergne TN
LVHW072116070426
835510LV00002B/77